STREET TALK

Ann Turner

Illustrations by Catherine Stock

Houghton Mifflin Company

Boston 1986

Library of Congress Cataloging in Publication Data

Turner, Ann Warren.
  Street talk.

  Summary: A collection of poems about city places and experiences.
    1. City and town life—Juvenile poetry.
  2. Children's poetry, American. [1. City and town
  life—Poetry. 2. American poetry] I. Stock,
  Catherine, ill. II. Title.
  PS3570.U665S7   1986   811'.54   85-27061
  ISBN 0-395-39971-8

Printed in the United States of America

V   10   9   8   7   6   5   4   3   2   1

Contents

The Zoo

The zoo is a wonderful place
if you like stinky birds,
elephants with baggy feet,
and snakes that kill
just by looking sideways.

I liked the place with the black light
and these little fuzz-its
crawled out of their holes
and blinked their purple eyes—
shiny and slow.

I liked the camel
with its wrinkled-up lip
and its "Hey, I'll stomp on you
if you move wrong" look,
kind of like Grandma
or my old teacher.

My favorite was the seal,
looked like nothin' ever bothered him,
slumped up like a sidewalk bag,
lyin' out in the sun
he only moved once—that's *my*
kind of animal.

Tom Cat

This cat, see, yellow
like an old man's eye,
slunk behind a garbage can
slam-rattle, slam-bang!
He pushed that lid off,
leapt inside,
tail whapped back and forth
and a sound like a kid's toy motor
started—stopped, started—stopped.

This kid came zap-dapping
down the street,
hat jammed on eyes,
shoulders hustling along,
he clamped that lid down tight,
kicked the can
and walked on out.

I waited 'til that busted
hat was gone
and tore that lid off—
I'm telling you
it was like lifting the top
of a spaghetti pot
with the steam puffing out.
That cat kept on roaring and purring,
the sound smoking up in the cold air,

I could've warmed my whole body.

Grandma

Grandma knows
all there is to know,
she told me so.
"I know long nights, child,
crickets creaking in the grass
and the smell of magnolias
so thick you could cut
a dress out of it."

"I know those old porches
and people sitting on 'em
talking babies, marriage, death
always one-two-three
with a joke about a man
and his woman, see,
after the death talk."

"And I know all
there is to know about babies—
teething, whining, colicky,
when to talk,
when to walk,
pat-patting their little backs."

"I'll tell you though
what I don't know—
how the rain comes up
so green and sudden,
why a woman ever says,
'I do'
and why men laugh so much
at those silly jokes."

Red-Dress Girl

The rope swings in
and out, sister dances
over the rope
her red dress flying,
and the feet in the sneakers go
spank-dab, spank-dab.

I got dizzy watching
she's so smooth
more like *she* stood still
and the rope flew round
her.

Mother called, "Come in."
She never minded,
her face calm
as an old moon
that red dress
flying.

The Museum

So we went to see this mummy
I'm telling you
dead for a ton of years,
so dead everything got used up
and there's only this paper shell
left with a nose pokin' out
and a wrinkled-up forehead
and these dry-whisper lips.

See, they put these magic charms
all over the body
to keep out those eat-'em-up devils,
there's a vulture and some
kind of snake,
a dog with spiky ears
and a dagger to fight
monsters with.

Hey, that's not such a bad
way to go except
I don't know if I want
fingers pokin' at me
a thousand years from now.

Don't Let Me

This empty man came, see,
with a body strung on bones
all stuffed in a bag of veins
and feet so slow I thought, God!
he's afraid he'll leak out.

And I said, Jesus!
Don't let me get old like that—
let me die fast-talking,
walking down night streets alive,
music on all sides.

But not dribble out,
not erase away (no mark left)
thankyouverymuch
sucked dry like a straw left
by some never-you-mind child.

Man

There's a next-door man
been around so long
his skin got polished
by all the summers and the winters
and he said, "Child,
you think it's hard now,
just wait 'til all those years
gang up on you
callin', tellin', naggin',

Did you do right?
Did you remember to?
Did you forget?
And you got to say,
I WAS BUSY
all those years, livin',
see—just livin'."

That's Gloria

Mr. MacGregor says
(how come their names
always sound like a college?),
"Be a secretary, Gloria,
you're quick and those fingers
are a way out."

What's that supposed to mean?
If I sit still and just move
my little fingers I'll be all right?
If I don't talk but just
tappity-tap-tap, I'm O.K.?

How does he get to know so much?
He doesn't know what's inside—
a swirling purple dress,
feet so light, arms
and hands that never make mistakes,
and a voice that makes your skin
ripple up—

that's Gloria!

Street Painting

I watched him a long time
and this is how he did it:
Stand in front of the wall
like it's a bad dream.
Make faces.
Jam your hat down.
Pull it off.
Pop your fingers—walk
around the block and come back,
start up like you surprised
the wall's still there.

Then sigh.
Take out your paints.
Doodle around with them,
stirring and humming.
Dip a brush in,
stare at it,
take a rush forward
and dab-dab-dab
at that wall.

Soon's you know,
you got faces
and bodies and trees
like they were locked up
in that old brush
and all you had to do
was stare at it
to get a picture.

Wash in the Street

I pass 'em
on my way to school
dumped like wash
in the street:
Gus and Bones and Sleepy
Maria

scrunched up on a bench
all their flapdoodle on—
gray, wrinkled socks,
a jacket drabby loose,
hats knit by trembly hands.

Once in a bus station I saw
a woman dressed like an opera,
a red turban on her head.
She sang so loud the pipes
hummed,
washing her purple feet
in the sink.

And people smile
or not
edge by like they're a dog
about to shake out all
its wet.

Night Roof

Steam—summer—steam
cook—August—cook
smoke—night—smoke.

People lie on roofs
talkin' and pokin' at the sky
like if you reached high
enough you'd poke through
and some of that silver light
would wash on down.

People lie on roofs
talkin' and singin'
sometimes a baby cries,
scared 'cause there's no ceiling
just this black empty sky
and someone says, "Look,
honey—stars, don't cry."

Here It Is

I love food
pizza-pepper plucking
at my throat
(hey-hot! hey-hot!),
fizzy Coke tickling
my nose (sssz-bam! sssz-bam!)
and a hamburger with all
the trimmings
slip-sliding out
when you munch down.

I love food
late at night
a crispy-crackly pack
of Doritos,
a fistful of Cheez Whiz,
a Twinkie soft and slinky.

But most I love
sitting at the table
with Ma frying bacon,

her steps whisp-shushing
back and forth, humming
(you can't *make* eggs right
without humming)
and she says, "Ben,
here it is,"

and there it is.

Red Flower

I went by this building,
brown, mostly gray
like all the city smoke
and noise got ground
into those bricks,
the window glass so black
it looked like tar.

And I thought, Nobody
lives there—too quiet,
too dark, too gray,
when I looked up and saw
one window open,
the curtains blowing in
and a red flower blooming.

25

The Park

One day I so depressed
I could hardly walk,
all the noise chokin'
my ears, the street smell
punchin' my nose,
I feel like a ball
being bounced around
by people's feet.

So I went to the park,
kicked a tree, spat
in a fountain and saw two kids
sitting on a rock,
and one said, "There's a giant
lives inside this tree
and a magic purple bird
and a fairy grandmother."

The other says, "What's
a fairy grandmother?" "Why,
they fly over you, take care
of your feet, pick you up
when you fall down."
The other smiled.
I walked slower
and looked up quick
in case I'd catch sight
of mine.

Look Up!

Do you ever see
how grown-ups don't look up
when they walk? They stare
at their feet,
the store windows,
some car they're mad at.

One day the taxi drivers
beeped and yelled,
people charged up the street
and I saw above

this huge gray bird
sailing along like we were the sea
and he looked for an island
to land on.

No one saw him,
no one but me and one
old lady who yelled, "Look,
everybody, look! A great blue
heron in New York!" I don't know
about no blue heron, but I do know
grown-ups need to look up
more.

Hello, Graffiti

The trains they come and go,
rattling, crashing through the dark
all their lights glowing
like a boat I heard of once
that rowed the dead
'cross a black river.

I step back
on the platform
afraid I'll jump in,
afraid someone'll PUSH
me in, it's so dark
and loud and wild.

Then the pictures
come shooting up—orange,
red and blue, SHAZAMM!
silver, gold, CRASH-BASH!
makes my heart beat
they're so light and cheery.

I step up
not afraid to ride on 'em
then.

Breakin'

There's a new beat
in the street
kids practicin' days
out of sight
to get it right explode
onto the square

rollin' on heads,
twirlin' on backs,
breakin' the turtle,
the baby, the back bridge
like they're a top—
makes the earth look soft
and the air easy.

And all the time they smile
or else look calm like some holy
men sayin' their prayers.

Voices

I love it when
we're curled up
and the night is
out of sight
behind curtains,
and Grandpa laughs
soft and slow.

The TV is like music,
people sit tellin' jokes
about lovers and jobs
and lucky numbers
and Momma slaps the chair
like it's a fresh person.

Late someone yawns,
another pulls on a coat
and the room empties out,
their voices floating up the stairs—

makes me happy
to hear those voices
after the faces
have gone away.

Halloween

A little kid
came to the door
dressed like a monster man;
eyes bugging out,
teeth fanging down,
nails like stabs
of white.

Then another came
dressed like a dance,
in purple tights,
flashy pants,
with a necklace jingle-
jangling.

I said, "Jeez!
Don't kids just put on
sheets anymore? Don't
they put on hats and be bums?
Why's everyone so fancy
all of a sudden?"

And they smiled slow
and said,
"You're just old,
too old to trick-or-treat.
Times've changed,
you know."

Sunday

Let me tell you
about church,
how people hold out
their hands and say,
"Hello!" folding you in
with their voices
like a soft blanket.

And the preacher shouts,
"Be good!" and I promise.
The songs are like fireworks,
then slow and easy—
makes you jump
then cry.

When you come out
you're new as a baby's skin
washed clean
for another day.

Amanda

This girl, Amanda,
I like a lot,
got eyes like sparkles
and a laugh
to make you warm.

She's smart, too,
knows those hard-to-find
answers,
"Steel, Mrs. Simms,"
"Akron, Ohio," and "Baby
whales are twelve feet long."

Thinks she keeps 'em
stored inside
like cans in a cupboard,
but better than smart
when she looks at me and smiles,
I don't care anymore
where Akron, Ohio, is.

Morning

Saw a play once,
the lights going down,
the talk shushed,
little bits of music starting up.

City's like that
early on,
dark, hushed streets,
stores with no lights,
trees like people, quiet
then

one man appears,
rattles up his burglar door,
steps in, steps out,
looks up and down the street,
invites the morning in.

Clean

When I was small
like five,
lived in a place
where they washed the streets.
I'd hear them at four
outside my window,
wheels rumble silent,
the swish of big brushes,
the hosing down—like steam.
And I'd think (but too
sleepy to do!)
about going out
and bouncing a red ball
down those streets,
just me—and the ball
on those clean,
sweet streets.

Read

Do you remember
learning to read?
That book full of squiggles
like ants escaped,
the teacher's big thumb
on the page,
your heart beating inside
afraid that all you'd ever see
was ants—

Then a word popped out,
"See," and another, "Cat,"
and my finger on teacher's,
we read, "I see cat."
I ran around the room
so happy I saw words
instead of ants.

Nowhere

There's a smell
that nowhere has
like the floor
of a bus station
speckled with cups,
like a locker left open
because nothing's *in* it,
like a pair of shoes
on a park bench
filled with rain,
like a tired gray ball
let out its tired gray air

that's the smell of nowhere.

People Leaves

People don't know city.
They say, city dark,
city drear,
no one can live here.
They don't know
how streets look
come morning,
like a tree let down
its sudden leaves.
That red-coat girl
splashed with white,
that man in a jump-up shirt of blue,
that woman wrapped in purple,
rolling her food home.
Wherever I look,
see people leaves
moving, drifting,
cheer my eyes.

Why?

Fumble-John they call him
lives in the place with no windows,
floors falling down,
doorway burned black,
sleeps on a bag,
gets warm by the trash can,
hardly eats — mostly drinks,
clothes look like they left
on the tracks and the trains
run back and over them,
so does the man.

And I wonder when I see him,
Who are his people?
Why is he here?
How did he get
so run over?

Teacher Talk

Teacher say, "Be what you can be."
"Do what you can do."
"Dream," she say.

I tell you what I dream.
That I walk down the street
and not look back.
That I go in a room
and no one stares.
That I sit at a table
and no one fights.
That I watch TV
and people are hugging.
That I hear on the radio
they *all* sit down
at a table to talk.

Then I can grow
then I can dream
then I can do.

The Beginning

This is where it begins
like God really lives in New York
and he opens his hands, PRESTO!
there are subway trains
   churning through the dark,
and Brooklyn Bridge swaying
   all its lights like ribbons,
and buildings climbing the sky
   the clouds just near,
and sea lapping the docks
   where men bellow and yell.

And there are children in parks
    always on swings,
and dogs running underfoot
    like bits of escaped rug,
and museums full of bones, birds,
    paintings and teeth—
long ago and here and always
    He said,
"Here's New York!"